INK GARDEN

Poems

Alexandria Ryu

CLAVIS & SOMNIUM

For the places that told me their stories...

Also for you, the reader.

Language's Travel

At first, I was born on Adam's lips and like you all,
written on earth then on stone slates,
dreaming of eternity.

I record the good, evil, and story of Genesis;
at times sit in encyclopedias in the name of Honor;
and sleep with Silence in all the books of the world.

My territory is in between those of Silence and Sound.

People name the incomprehensible, with me, fate;
call God, who is around us, with me, love;
and say pain is God's face.

My longtime companion was papyrus
and today, on the third day of January 2000 AD,
I travel at the speed of light.

People call it hope or despair
but it's just a romantic trip for me.

Genghis Khan Airport

10,000 feet above the Great Wall of China,
aren't life and death just like this?

Like the landscape that fades as altitude rises,
I'll forget this life's memories and be reborn.

I thought, as I gazed at the 50,000th wildflower on the
meadow,
past life's relations,
this life's relations,
next life's relations,
all transient, like smoke.

Foggy Day

On a foggy day,
on the back of a rented horse,
on my way to Khan's tomb,
I thought,
I forgot how to fly
as I learned to walk on Earth.
Have I been walking for too long?
Will I be able to fly again?

Like the men who keep the world in their hearts,
a day here has the four seasons.

The meadow glows cobalt-blue during the day,
smiles with several faces from white to black,
and holds up a night sky; it's pouring stars.

Freedom

I lock my eyes with the horizon across the plain.

I think,
I've been primping too much,
wearing too much makeup,
far too much self-conscious,
living like an idiot.

I've even been to, with Khan's army,
to the German feudal estates.

Now I'm locked up in a small cage in the Far East,
weeping quietly.

A Persian cat snoozes in a sunlit rooftop apartment.
A child grooms her, feeds her, and asks, "Are you happy?"

She smells freedom in her dreams.
The eternally unforgettable
scent from the Emperor's palace.

Hour between Dog and Wolf

Like the yaks that never leave
their Himalayan homeland,
wolves stay in the forest, the feral forest.
People who became dogs
only remember the forest they left
when they are castrated and discarded.
I should head for the forest,
into the scent of wild grass.

...

There, I will rise when the sun rises,
fall asleep when the sun sets,
and gaze at the dewdrops
forming and evaporating
very slowly.

À la Ladakh

On the day I lose my phone, I decide to live à la Ladakh:
write a letter on paper,
go to the post office,
wait for his reply for a long time,
appreciate a meal a day and a few clothes,
be grateful for having been born as a human,
read the Tibetan Book of the Dead,
buy vegetables from an old street vendor,
and save a bee's life.

On the day I lose my wallet, I decide to live à la Ladakh:
plant a seed,
wait for a long time,
and share the fruit with a worm.

Wilderness Area

When I was silence, arctic moss, a wooden fence covered with rose vines, a deer's eyes, a baby's first inhalation, the first budding leaf of a wild rose shrub, a bucket in a deep well, and a sentence in the 14th century's letter.

When I was shade in a forest, a passing season, a coyote's howling, a thread of the Maya civilization, and a lark on a redwood branch.

When universes disappear every minute,
when I go back to silence.

Charity Box

Dropping unused clothes in the charity box,
I think of the Tibetan children in tattered clothes
with clear eyes.

Do we need fancy clothes
to hide our tattered souls?

Some people don't need luxury clothing.

Reading

To read is
for one person
to soliloquize before a monochrome background
and for another
to listen in a sunlit study.

Sometimes
to speak different languages
but nonetheless
to understand each other
and
to walk the forest of souls
next to each other.

Gravestone

Passing by, the wind reads a gravestone:

Here lies the free soul
who was never tamed
or caged
or defined by a name,
who never bought fame
sacrificing her freedom.

Istanbul

The sound of prayers fills the air.
A woman hurries through a shaded alley.
In Istanbul's red-light district is a girl
who'll kill you if you don't promise her
love.

Silk Road

In one eye, Asia;
in the other, Europe.

In one ear, whimpers;
in the other, laughter.

Open my eyes, colors;
close my eyes, truth.

In June, days and nights chase one another.

I turn into a different woman
as I fly through each time zone
7,000 feet above the Silk Road.

India

I go to India.
I go to the land of the people
who say their own words
and believe in their own gods.

Worrying I might bother them
with my second-vertebra-broken,
quadriplegic soul
clad in rags called modernity,
I go past the Karakoram Highway
into the scent of Ayurveda.

North Han River

It has been a trip from the source to estuary,
from oxygen and green to the gray sky.

Now is time to go back.

There, they look into each other
and ask, "Are you okay?"
Raindrops, snowflakes, fog particles.

Near the sea, waves are gentle.
I will lose myself but wear peace,
toss and turn in oceans for a few centuries,
sleep in a tree for a hundred years,
live freely in a transparent body,
and fall on that valley where
there's nothing but oxygen and green.

Metaphysical Conversation

Now is time for you and me.
Nothing can interfere with us.
Not even fame or blood.

Your silence and my tears are
our last conversation.

Whenever I look at
Chuncheon's clear sky,
I'll think of it as your heart.

A bird's song, your voice.
Falling snow, your soul.
The long river, our friendship.

Waypoint

The car navigation system,
equipped with the latest artificial intelligence,
keeps leading me to a town
past the highway and provincial roads,
persistently.

"Soon, turn right."
"You have abandoned the path."
"Soon, make a U-turn."

There's no road.
Still it tells me to go.

Maybe it's right.
Maybe we have abandoned the path.

For we no longer hear
what morning tells us,
what summer tells us,
what our hearts tell us,
what cats tell us,
or what love tells us.

Explorer

He keeps silent for several seasons.
In my mind, hundreds of questions
that I don't ask.

Instead, I go to Machu Picchu,
explore the Amazon rainforest,
and stay in Marrakech.

I return to my own life before love.

I go back to my 20-year-old self,
plan my life again,
keep an ambitious dream,
and become stronger and wiser.

But at times,
I still write letters
that I never send to him.

That his silence is
Terra Nova.

Bread and Roses

As I make breakfast,
dewdrops evaporate.

As I make lunch,
the sun's strongest rays wane.

As I make dinner,
morning glories close.

I couldn't grow roses
because I had to bake bread.

But I will still think of it as a rosy life.

Phantom Pain

As fairy tales begin and end,
as roses bloom and wither,
as dewdrops appear and disappear,
a nameless flower blooms.

Our love is complicated.
Under the charm of time
you're prettier than a snowflake
but will disappear sooner.

Colors fade in fallen rose petals.

Only you can turn this rain into sunlight.
Only you can turn these sobs into Christmas chimes.
Only you can be the pastel tones for my sad mornings.

But do you really exist?

Royalties

I buy poetry to endure my time on Earth.
Now royalties will cross the borders.

A dollar to Sichuan
A dollar to Northern Song
A dollar to the 19th-century Kyoto
A dollar to an Indian reservation
A dollar into the Siberian snowstorm
A dollar for a radish or a cabbage
A dollar for the 10 autumns in a poetry collection.
A dollar for the 10 winters in a novel.
A dollar for a cup of coffee.
A dollar for a rose.

We navigate through the storm of neoliberalism
on a small boat with the 15th century's wages.

New Morning

A new morning comes.
Something is different.
The humidity is different.
The light's angles are different.
My anatomy is different.

A new evening comes.
Partly from the past.
Partly from the future.
My heart's hues are different.

A new love comes.
They say,
a person loves as much as their heart is wide.
Love as big as a handful of sunlight.
Downpour-like love.
Blizzard-like love.

Sometimes we weigh love.
The heavier one kills the lighter one.

Tomorrow comes anew.

Escapism

I escaped the Child Station
I was so tall, the world was as big as a marble.
An angel still held my hand, keeping darkness at bay.

I escaped the First Love Station.
Such a strange experience,
a man's face and the color of his T-shirt
painted themselves all over the world.
I also realized: heaven and hell, look alike.

I escaped the Mother Station.
Time for journaling,
time for quiet walks,
an apt waistline,
and lethal love,
all exchanged for the title called Mother.

I escaped the Woman Station
I am no longer visible
like a falling leaf,
like the wind,
like a snowflake,
like the sound of a passing season.

No, I just escaped all that.
It's a picture from the heart
for the original has passed.

Ink Garden

I lost the path leading to the world and
followed the one into books instead.
It led me to a quiet place.
I'd rather stay here, for a lifetime.

There was a girl who dreamt of
a garden made of ink.
She did not forget the dream for
several lifetimes and
wrote it down in her first diary of
each life.

Leaves bud on a tree drawn in ink.
A bird sits on a branch.

Globe

Turning a globe,
one second suffices from Seoul to Los Angeles:
the distance of a palm.

Half a second to Hawaii.
A yacht floats on white foam.

A third of a palm to the Taj Mahal.

A palm and a half to Amsterdam.
People drink stars in Café Orange.

A palm to the North Pole.
A sled runs.
One of the dogs has a hurting leg.

An arm to the moon.

Two arms to a star.

A person's height to the Andromeda Galaxy.

To eternity ... how far?

House

At the house, I could hear the sound of snow
and tell the size of the flakes.
I could hear the snow stop falling.

I could hear the rain
and tell the size of the drops, too.

I could hear the moss roses germinate
and bloom on the flowerbed.

I could sense the frost rising.

I awoke and fell asleep every day,
feeling the sun rise and set.
Sometimes, the sun set late,
gazing at the flowerbed.

Sometimes,
a deer traversed the two-lane road
in front of the house
among the mountains.

Summertime, we played house.
Last year's autumn stole glimpses
hiding in shade
and vanished when discovered, startled.

Silence gazed at us under the moss rose leaves.

When a meal of grass and earth was made,
The sun paid a visit too.

Bored, we scrapped everything
and played marbles, hopscotch;
dusk fell when we got to hide and seek.

Funeral

His heart stops beating.

The love of your life, sudden discomfort.
You keep him in a refrigerator,
burn him hurriedly,
crush his ashes mercilessly
and send him to the wind.

How come? You used to love him.
You couldn't live without him.

He is locked up on the 10th floor,
just as when he was alive.
The only difference: he's in an urn.
Wait, another: he is exempt from commute.

He who died
talks to his family,
hugs his family,
and watches himself burn.

Springcreek

On an autumnal day like this,
I lose the path to the world,
counting colored leaves.

On an autumnal day like this,
I ponder the ancient beings
in the colored forest.

On an autumnal day like this,
I decide to visit Chuncheon and complete my poetry.

Do you know how beautiful Chuncheon is,
seen through the rainwater on the windshield?
Once seen, unforgettable. You can't leave either.

A river runs next to me, listening to my life stories.
The mountain's shadow embraces me.
Time for recovery.
I plunge into the river of time
and look at the currents.

There, I will look into my wound which will have been
exposed by a raindrop,
permeated by fog,
and touched by a snowflake;
play with language;
then fall asleep.

I will ripen like the oak in an uncharted forest.

I need no worldly reputation,
but sunlight, rain, and Earth's lips.

Should I add one more,
a staff of whistles from a passing stranger.

Mountain

From a snowy mountain,
a yak gazes at the meadows below.

It sits on a school's rooftop
and stands by the Library of Alexandria
with Reinhold Messner.

A crystal-like blizzard rages.
Like the mule ambling on the Karakoram Highway,
I amble in between letters.

A man gazes at the sky and land alternatingly,
pondering whether to belong in the world
or bury himself in silence.

I take out photos from the album of my future.
My next life's face overlaps on my face
on a train's window on the Trans-Siberian Railway,
in a hut on the Tibetan high grounds,
and on the Mongolian meadows.

I will leave this life's memories here.

A small noise can trigger a snowslide there,
burying many souls.

People never know.
Birds leave, trees die, and snow melts away.

...

I have a dream:
to go past the Karakoram Highway
and complete my life in the Himalayas.

To find the deepest crevice
among God's skyscrapers.

Rain

Rain brings ancient memories
to a corner of my journal, without anyone's knowing.
It must have acquired feelings
after millions of years of existence.

Drizzle guards my dreams, careful not to wake me.

Fog rises from water to tell me,
"Love is a memory from the past life."

Downpour thrives to emphasize a landscape.

Rainstorm rages to erase the world's scribbles
and drown out its noise, when I'm tired.

Frost covers earth to give it a break
from all the bearing of its green children.

Snow falls to tell me,
"Time transmutes sorrow into a gemstone of the soul."

To Be a Poet

To be a poet is
to count the rings of
a fallen redwood.

To be a poet is
to pay my respects
to a seashell grave in the Himalayas.

To be a poet is
to remember heaven's language until I die.

To be a poet is
to remember the heartbeats of my first love.

To be a poet is
to gaze into a cat's eyes
that become two gemstones
when the sun rises.

To be a poet is
to be solitary and silent.

To be a poet is
to forever stay as Slowness and Nothing's
best friend.

Thank you for reading!

Thank you for reading my poems. It truly means a lot to me. I thank you, from the bottom of my heart. If you liked the book, please kindly leave a review. Thank you.

Feelings and thoughts taste better when shared. Share your feelings and thoughts on this book with your loved ones!

About the Author

Alexandria Ryu travels the world and writes about what it tells her. She was born in a deep mountain village in Korea. She was submerged in green and breathed it as she grew up. Green became part of her soul. Now she writes about it in her diary as poems. *Ink Garden* is her first poetry collection. You can follow her on Instagram (@alexandriaryu).

Copyright © 2017 Alexandria Ryu
Published by Clavis & Somnium
Cover image © Jay Mantri
Typeface "Open Sans" © Steve Matteson
Typeface "Spectral" © Production Type
ISBN: 9791196148720